Extreme Rock Climbing Moves

By Kathleen W. Deady

Consultants:
Shawn and Steve Allen
Boardmembers
United States Competition Climbing
Association (USCCA)

CAPSTONE
HIGH-INTEREST
BOOKS

an imprint of Capstone Press
Mankato, Minnesota

Capstone High-Interest Books are published by Capstone Press
151 Good Counsel Drive, P.O. Box 669, Mankato, Minnesota 56002
http://www.capstone-press.com

Library of Congress Cataloging-in-Publication Data
Deady, Kathleen W.
    Extreme rock climbing moves / by Kathleen W. Deady.
    v. cm.—(Behind the moves)
    Includes bibliographical references (p. 31) and index.
    Contents: Extreme rock climbing—Face climbing moves—Crack climbing moves—Safe
rock climbing—Extreme rock climbing slang.
    ISBN 0-7368-1514-7 (hardcover)
    1. Rock climbing—Juvenile literature. 2. Extreme sports—Juvenile literature. [1. Rock
climbing. 2. Extreme sports.] I. Title. II. Series.
GV200.2 .D43 2003
796.52'23—dc21   2002008180

Summary: Discusses the sport of rock climbing, including the hand and foot moves rock
climbers perform, rock climbing competitions, and safety concerns.

Editorial Credits
Carrie Braulick, editor; Karen Risch, product planning editor; Kia Adams,
    series designer; Molly Nei, book designer; Jo Miller, photo researcher

Photo Credits
Aurora/Gabe Palacio, 12, 14
Corbis/Duomo, cover, 28; Galen Rowell, 4, 7, 16, 19, 22, 27; Adam Woolfitt, 9;
    Tom Stewart, 10; Neil Rabinowitz, 20
Getty Images/Nate Bilow, 16 (inset); Mike Powell, 24
PhotoDisc, Inc., 4 (inset), 10 (inset), 24 (inset)

1 2 3 4 5 6 08 07 06 05 04 03

Table of Contents

Free climbers use ropes and harnesses.

Learn about:

■ Types of rock climbing

■ Climbing equipment

■ Competitions

Chapter One

Extreme Rock Climbing

Many people think Lynn Hill is one of the best rock climbers in the United States. She has completed some of the hardest climbs in the world and has won more than 30 international competitions.

Hill is best known for making the first free climb of the El Capitan nose route in less than one day. El Capitan is a cliff in California's Yosemite National Park. The top of the nose route is more than 3,000 feet (914 meters) high. Hill completed this route in 1994.

Types of Rock Climbing

Around the 1930s, mountain climbers became interested in rock climbing as a sport. Before this time, most people only climbed rocks to practice. Their main goal was to climb high mountains.

Today, rock climbing is popular. Rock climbers can choose between several types of climbing. Many people enjoy bouldering. Boulderers climb on large rocks that are low to the ground. The rocks usually are less than 12 feet (3.7 meters) high. Climbers do not need ropes or any other safety equipment except a pad. The climbers can fall onto the pad at the end of the climb without seriously hurting themselves.

Free climbers climb taller rock faces. Many of these rocks are more than 1,000 feet (305 meters) high. Free climbers use safety gear to protect themselves if they fall. This equipment includes a rope attached to a piece of webbed nylon called a harness.

Traditional climbers use ropes and harnesses as free climbers do. But they also place various objects into rocks to protect themselves. They call the objects "protection." A climber attaches the rope to the protection. The protection prevents the climber from falling long distances. Some traditional climbers place wedge-shaped objects called camming devices into cracks as protection.

Many people sport climb. Sport climbers often climb on artificial walls in indoor climbing gyms or on natural rock faces outdoors. The walls or rock faces have permanent bolts with hangers as protection. Sport climbers attach their ropes to the hangers as they climb.

Boulderers climb on rocks low to the ground.

Lead Climbing and Top Roping

Climbers can choose to lead climb or top rope. Both methods require two people. One person climbs. The other person is called the belayer. Belayers hold one end of the rope to prevent climbers from falling long distances. The rope is passed through a belaying device. This device grips the rope tightly to help the belayer support the climber's weight.

Lead climbers use pieces of nylon webbing called quickdraws to attach their ropes to protection as they climb a rock. Quickdraws have a D-shaped metal ring called a carabiner on each end.

Rock climbers who top rope put their ropes through an anchor at the top of climbing walls or rocks before they begin climbing. The anchor must support climbers during falls. Anchors often are carabiners attached to bolts.

Competitions

Rock climbing competitions are popular worldwide. The United States Competition Climbing Association (USCCA) holds many climbing competitions throughout the United States.

Expert climbers can compete in the X Games and the World Cup. Top athletes from around the world compete in these events.

Belayers stand on the ground and hold one end of the rope.

Climbers sometimes use ledges as handholds.

Learn about:

Rock features

Footwork

Using the hands and arms

Chapter Two

Face Climbing Moves

Rock climbers use many moves and skills to climb rock faces. Rock faces often are smooth, with few places to hold. Climbers keep their weight balanced over their feet. They try to stay close to the rock. Gravity pushes their weight down into their shoes. The contact between the shoes and the rock creates a force called friction. The friction gives the climbers' feet a good grip.

Rock climbers look closely at the rock surface for holds on which to place their hands and feet. Holds may be large surfaces that jut out from the face. Holds also can be slight dents, rough spots, or uneven areas. Climbers use different foot and hand moves for different holds.

To edge, climbers place their foot on a small bump.

Footwork

Climbers use various foot positions. They may use a foot position called a smear on a rounded bump. They press the sole of their shoe against the rock to help hold the foot in place.

Climbers may use a move called edging on some holds. They place the edge of their shoe on a bump in the rock face. Climbers usually use the edge of the shoe along the big toe. Climbers also may use the front edge of the shoe. This move is called toeing-in.

Advanced rock climbers sometimes use the heel hook. They kick a foot up or out to hook a hold with their heel. Climbers then pull themselves up with the foot that is hooked around the hold to reach a handhold. Climbers also kick a foot out to catch a hold with their toe. This move is called toe hooking.

Handholds and Arm Moves

Climbers use many hand grips. They often use an open grip on large, rounded holds called slopers. They place their whole hand around the hold. On small holds, climbers may use a crimp or a pinch grip. To perform a crimp grip, climbers grasp the hold with their fingertips. In a pinch grip, they pinch the hold with their thumb and index finger.

Climbers use only their fingers on some handhold

Climbers undercling by grabbing holds with their palms facing up. Climbers then pull up and out while leaning back. This action pushes the feet down harder on the rock.

Climbers often use a movement called the mantle to move up onto a narrow ledge or flat area. Climbers hold the ledge with one hand while placing their feet as high as possible. They lift their body up to put the other palm down on the ledge. They pull one leg onto the ledge. They then pull up the other leg to stand on the ledge.

Other Movements

Climbers use many body movements. They may bounce or leap to reach a hold. These movements are called dynoing. Climbers also may need to stretch or twist their bodies to reach a hold.

Large, overhanging rocks sometimes stick out from rock faces. Climbers must have great strength and use advanced foot and hand moves to climb around an overhang. They sometimes move upside-down to get around an overhang.

Learn about:

- **Finger cracks**

- **Hand and fist cracks**

- **Chimneys**

Chapter Three

Crack Climbing Moves

Rock climbers use cracks in rock surfaces to help them climb. These cracks may be tiny splits or wide gaps in the rock.

Finger Cracks

Rock climbers place their fingers into small cracks. Climbers may try to get as many fingers into a crack as possible. Sometimes they can fit all their fingers in a crack. Other times, they can fit only the tip of the pinkie finger in a crack.

Climbers move their fingers into different positions until they fit into the crack. Climbers sometimes pull their fingers down. The knuckles then fit tightly in the crack.

Hand and Fist Cracks

Some cracks are too wide for fingers. Climbers may jam one of their hands into a crack. Climbers move their hands in different ways depending on the size of a crack. Climbers may fold a thumb across the palm. This movement widens the hand so it jams into the crack. Climbers usually bend their knuckles at the base of the hand to make it fit tightly in a crack.

Climbers may place a fist in large cracks. They first relax the fist and put it into the crack. They then flex the fist to make it fit tightly.

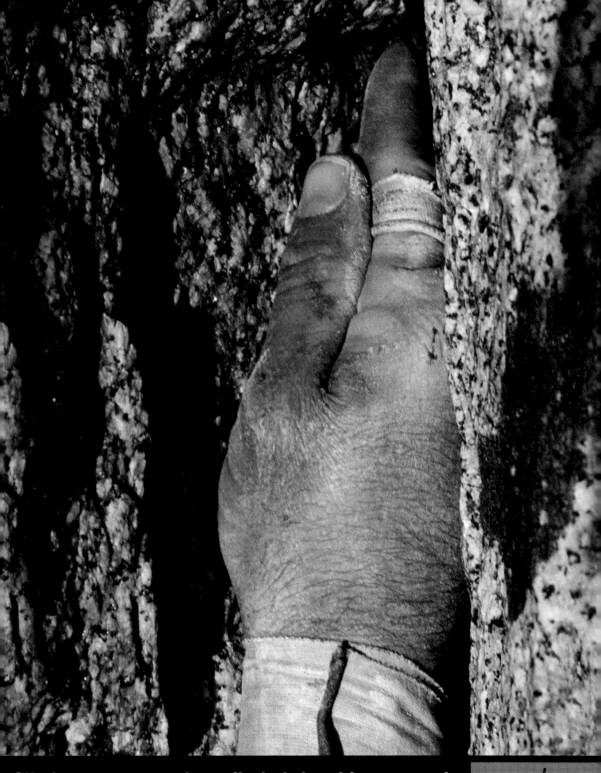

Climbers can sometimes fit their hand into a crack.

19

Climbers can fit their whole body in chimneys.

Off-Width Cracks and Chimneys

Some cracks are too wide to jam a fist inside, but too narrow for the whole body. Climbers call these off-width cracks.

To move up off-width cracks, climbers turn sideways toward the crack. They put one arm and one foot inside the crack. They press the palm inside the crack forward against the rock. They push back with the upper arm and elbow. They also press the inside knee and foot against the rock. Climbers then use their other leg and foot to move upward.

Climbers can sometimes fit their whole body into a crack. They call these cracks chimneys. Climbers press against the front wall of the chimney with their knees. They press against the back wall with their back. They keep the soles of their shoes flat against the back wall to increase friction. Climbers then press their hands forward to steady themselves as they move up the chimney.

Extreme Rock Climbing Slang

barndoor—to swing off a rock after losing the foot or handholds on one side of the body

bomber—a reliable piece of protection or anchor

comp—an organized sport climbing competition

flash—to complete a climb without falling

hangdog—to rest by hanging on the rope

mojo—a state of mind that helps climbers overcome problems

screamer—a long fall during which the climber screams

whipper—a long fall during a lead climb due to slack in the rope

zipper—to rip out several protections while falling

Climbers use hand chalk to improve their grip.

Learn about:

Safety equipment

Safety practices

Indoor climbing walls

Chapter Four

Safety

Rock climbers follow basic safety rules. They use equipment made especially for climbing. Climbers take good care of their gear. They make sure it is in good condition before and after each climb.

Safety Gear

Climbers use a variety of equipment to keep safe. They use nylon ropes and harnesses. The nylon in this equipment stretches slightly to prevent injury to climbers if they fall.

Many rock climbers wear helmets. Helmets protect the head during a fall. They also can protect a climber's head from falling objects.

Climbers use shoes made just for rock climbing. These shoes have a stiff, sticky rubber sole. They protect climbers' feet and help create friction. The shoes fit tightly on climbers' feet. This feature helps climbers control their footwork.

Outdoor climbers make sure they dress properly according to weather conditions. They may layer their clothes to keep themselves warm during cold weather. They wear waterproof clothing in rainy weather.

Many climbers carry hand chalk. The chalk keeps climbers' hands dry to prevent slipping.

any climbers wear helmets to protect their head.

Many competitions take place at indoor climbing gyms

Indoor Climbing Walls

In the past, people rock climbed only on natural outdoor rock faces. In the 1980s, many people started to climb on artificial climbing walls in indoor gyms. The holds on artificial walls are similar to the holds on real rocks. Today, many North American cities have climbing gyms with artificial walls.

Climbers on indoor walls can reduce their risk of injury. Rock climbers can practice difficult moves on indoor walls. They then will be prepared to use the moves on a natural rock face. Climbers also can use indoor walls during bad weather conditions. Bad weather conditions can make outdoor climbing dangerous. Trained climbers often are available to teach beginning climbers at indoor gyms. Others are available to help climbers if they become injured.

Rock climbers work to keep their sport safe. They know that using the proper gear and climbing in a safe environment are ways they can reduce the risks of their sport.

Words to Know

belayer (bi-LAY-ur)—a person who secures a climber's rope; the belayer helps prevent the climber from falling long distances.

carabiner (kar-a-BEE-nur)—a metal ring that climbers use to hold equipment together

chimney (CHIM-nee)—a crack large enough to fit a climber's whole body

friction (FRIK-shuhn)—the force created when one object rubs against another object

protection (proh-TEK-shun)—the equipment that climbers place in rocks; climbers attach their ropes to protection.

quickdraw (KWIK-draw)—a piece of nylon webbing that has a carabiner attached to each end

To Learn More

Champion, Neil. *Rock Climbing.* Radical Sports. Chicago: Heinemann, 2000.

Ryan, Pat. *Rock Climbing.* World of Sports. Mankato, Minn.: Smart Apple Media, 2000.

Voeller, Edward A. *Sport Climbing.* Extreme Sports. Mankato, Minn.: Capstone Press, 2000.

Useful Addresses

The Alpine Club of Canada
Indian Flats Road
P.O. Box 8040
Canmore, AB T1W 2T8
Canada

American Alpine Club
710 10th Street
Suite 100
Golden, CO 80401

United States Competition Climbing Association
P.O. Box 502568
Indianapolis, IN 46250

Internet Sites

Track down many sites about rock climbing.
Visit the FACT HOUND at *http://www.facthound.com*

IT IS EASY! IT IS FUN!

1) Go to http://www.facthound.com
2) Type in: 0736815147
3) Click on "FETCH IT" and FACT HOUND will find
   several links hand-picked by our editors.

Relax and let our pal FACT HOUND do the research for you!

Index